Resilient Faith

Finding Strength in Christ Through the Stories of the Faithful

by
Risa Stegall

The Shepherd's Word Publishing

Resilient Faith: Finding Strength in Christ Through the Stories of the Faithful

© 2025 Risa Stegall

All rights reserved. No part of this book may be reproduced in any form or by any electronic or mechanical means including information storage and retrieval systems, without permission in writing from the publisher, except by a reviewer who may quote brief passages in a review.

Scripture quotations are taken from the Holy Bible, New International Version®, NIV®. Copyright ©1973, 1978, 1984, 2011 by Biblica, Inc.™ Used by permission. All rights reserved worldwide.

First Edition: 2025
ISBN: **979-8-9988435-2-5**

Published by Shepherd's Word Publishing
Printed in the United States of America
First Edition

Dedication

I dedicate this book to my mother,
whose unwavering faith and quiet strength shaped the foundation of my life,
and to everyone who has weathered storms,
stood firm in the face of adversity,
and continues to walk in resilient faith.

May these words remind you that through every trial,
God's grace is more than sufficient.

Table of Contents

- Introduction
- Joseph — Purpose Through Pain
- Job — Unshakable Faith
- David — Courage in Crisis
- Esther — Risk with Righteousness
- Paul — Strength Under Pressure
- Ruth — Loyalty in Loss
- Daniel — Integrity Under Fire
- Nehemiah — Vision Amid Opposition
- Hannah — Patient Hope
- Peter — Restoration After Failure
- Moses — Leadership in the Wilderness
- Jesus — Endurance for Glory
- Conclusion: Living a Resilient Faith
- 7-Day Resilience Devotional
- 30 Scriptures for Resilient Faith
- Acknowledgments
- About the Author

Introduction

Resilient Faith: Standing Strong Through Life's Trials and Triumphs

---

There are moments in life that test us beyond what we thought we could endure.

Moments that leave us breathless — not because of awe, but because of heartbreak.
Moments when strength seems to evaporate and hope feels like a distant memory.

And yet, it is in these very moments that resilience is born.

Resilience is not the absence of struggle — it is the presence of unwavering faith in the midst of it.
It is the quiet courage to believe that God's promises are still true when everything around us seems to collapse.
It is the determination to get up, not because we feel strong, but because we know *He* is.

In a world that measures success by speed, fame, and fortune, God measures it differently.
He measures it by endurance. By perseverance.
By the ability to stand firm, to remain unshaken, and to trust Him through every storm.

The Bible is filled with stories of men and women who learned resilience not in comfort, but in crisis.
They were not perfect. They questioned, doubted, even stumbled — but they refused to quit.
Their lives show us that resilience is not about never falling — it's about always rising again, anchored in God's grace.

This book is a journey through the lives of twelve such individuals. Ordinary people who faced extraordinary trials — and who, by God's power, endured.

Through their stories, you will discover:

- How Joseph rose from the pit to the palace.
- How Job worshiped in the ashes of loss.
- How Esther found courage when silence could have meant death.
- How Paul pressed on through beatings, shipwrecks, and betrayal.
- How Jesus endured the cross, despising its shame, for the joy set before Him.

Each chapter will invite you to see resilience not as a human achievement but as a divine partnership.
You will learn that God does not call you to be strong in yourself — He calls you to be strong *in Him*.
You will find encouragement to face your own trials with a new perspective — one that says,
"I am pressed, but not crushed. Persecuted, but not abandoned. Struck down, but not destroyed." (2 Corinthians 4:8-9)

At the end of each chapter, you will find:

- **Declarations** to speak life and truth over your situation,
- **Prayers** to invite God's strength into your weakness,
- **Challenges** to put your faith into action.

And as you walk through this journey, you'll also find a **7-Day Resilience Devotional** — a focused time to reset, rebuild, and refocus your heart on God's promises.

This is not a book to merely read — it is a book to *live*.

It is a call to resilient faith.

Not a brittle, breakable faith.
Not a faith that bends with every wind of adversity.
But a faith that stands firm — *rooted in God's unchanging love, empowered by His Spirit,* and *anchored in the hope of His promises.*

No matter what you are facing today, know this:

You were made to endure.
You were made to overcome.
You were made to rise again.

Welcome to *Resilient Faith*.

Let's begin.

Chapter 1: Joseph — Purpose Through Pain

Pillar of Resilience: God's Purpose Prevails

Imagine being thrown into a pit by your own brothers.
The very people you loved — the ones you trusted — stripped you of your robe and your dignity.
You cry out, but no one answers. You reach up, but no one pulls you out.
Sold as a slave, betrayed again, falsely accused, and forgotten in prison.

Joseph's life, at first glance, reads more like a tragedy than a triumph.

But Joseph's story teaches us one of the greatest truths about resilience:
Your pain does not cancel God's purpose — it fulfills it.

Joseph's resilience was not rooted in revenge, bitterness, or self-pity. It was rooted in a deep, unshakable trust in the sovereignty of God. Joseph understood what many of us must learn — that when life feels out of control, God is still in control.

Genesis 50:20 records Joseph's words to the very brothers who betrayed him:

"You intended to harm me, but God intended it for good to accomplish what is now being done, the saving of many lives." (Genesis 50:20, NIV)

Joseph's trials prepared him for his destiny.
His time in the pit prepared him for leadership in Pharaoh's palace.
His time in prison refined his character to steward great influence without pride.

What others meant for evil; God used for good.
Joseph's life is a powerful reminder that pain is often the birthplace of purpose.

Life Application

When life falls apart, it is easy to ask:

"Why is this happening to me?"

Joseph's story challenges us to ask instead:

"God, what are You preparing me for?"

Resilience grows when we stop seeing our suffering as pointless and start seeing it as preparation.

Pain is not wasted in God's hands.
Delayed dreams are not denied dreams.
Every betrayal, every disappointment, every lonely night — God uses them to forge strength, character, and readiness in us.

When you face betrayal or hardship, remember:

- You are not buried; you are planted.
- Growth is happening in the dark.
- Purpose is being born in silence.

Declaration of Resilience

Today, I declare:
"What was meant for my harm, God is turning for my good.
My setbacks are setups for divine purpose.

I will not quit, I will not break — I am being prepared for greater things.
In Jesus' name, Amen."

Prayer

Father God,
When I cannot see the way forward, help me trust that You are still working behind the scenes.
Give me the resilience to endure seasons of betrayal, disappointment, and delay.
Turn my pain into preparation, my trials into testimony, and my hardships into hallways toward Your destiny for me.
Strengthen my faith so that I do not grow weary in doing good, knowing that at the proper time, I will reap a harvest if I do not give up.
In Jesus' name, Amen.

Resilience Challenge

- Reflect on a painful season of your life.
- Write down **one lesson** you learned through it that you wouldn't have gained any other way.
- This week, *speak Genesis 50:20 over your situation*: *"What was meant for harm, God is using for good."*

Reflections: Joseph

Take a few moments to reflect on what God has spoken to you through this chapter.

- What is one lesson from Joseph's life that you can apply to your current situation?
- Where is God calling you to trust His purpose even when the path is painful?
- What personal declaration can you make based on Joseph's journey of resilience?

Chapter 2: Job — Unshakeable Faith

Pillar of Resilience: Worshiping Through the Storm

Picture a man who had it all — wealth, family, influence, and respect. In a moment, he loses everything. His children are gone. His wealth is wiped away. His health is broken.
Friends blame him. His wife tells him to curse God and die.
Job finds himself sitting in ashes, scraping his wounds with broken pottery.

And yet — **Job worshiped**.

Job's life teaches us a deeper dimension of resilience:
True faith is not measured by what we have but by who we trust when all is taken away.

Job 1:20-21 records one of the most staggering acts of faith in all of Scripture:

"At this, Job got up and tore his robe and shaved his head. Then he fell to the ground in worship and said: 'Naked I came from my mother's womb, and naked I will depart. The Lord gave and the Lord has taken away; may the name of the Lord be praised.'" (Job 1:20-21, NIV)

Job's resilience was not in pretending he wasn't hurting — it was in **worshiping while he was wounded.**
It was not a denial of pain; it was a declaration of trust.

He understood that worship is not reserved for the mountaintops — it is most powerful in the valleys.
When everything else crumbles, resilient faith says:

"Though He slay me, yet will I hope in Him." (Job 13:15)

Life Application

We often believe that resilience means *being strong*.
But sometimes, resilience means *bowing low in surrender*.

Job teaches us:

- It's okay to grieve — but grieve *with hope*.
- It's okay to question — but question *in faith*.
- It's okay to hurt — but *worship in the hurting*.

Your resilience will not be measured by how loudly you shout on the good days,
but by how faithfully you whisper His name on the hard days.

Declaration of Resilience

Today, I declare:
"The Lord is my strength and my song.
Even in loss, I will praise Him.
My faith is not built on what God gives, but on who God is.
I will worship in the waiting, trust through the trial, and hope in His goodness.
In Jesus' name, Amen."

Prayer

Father God,
When life shatters my plans, let my heart still sing Your praises.
Teach me to trust You not just for what You give, but for who You are.
Strengthen me to worship in seasons of weeping and to stand firm when my world is shaken.
Let my life be a testimony that You are worthy of praise — in every season, through every storm.
In Jesus' name, Amen.

Resilience Challenge

- Take five minutes today to *worship God* — not for what He has done, but for who He is.
- List three attributes of God (His goodness, His faithfulness, His mercy) and thank Him for each.
- Speak Job 13:15 aloud:
  "Though He slay me, yet will I hope in Him."

Reflections: Job

Take a few moments to reflect on what God has spoken to you through this chapter.

- What is one lesson from Job's life that you can apply to your current situation?
- Where is God asking you to worship even through your suffering?
- What personal declaration can you make based on Job's journey of resilience?

Chapter 3: David — Courage in Crisis

Pillar of Resilience: Trusting God in the Wilderness

Imagine being anointed king — and then spending years running for your life.
Hiding in caves. Living as a fugitive. Betrayed by friends. Hunted by a king whose throne you are destined to inherit.

David knew what it meant to live between **the promise and the palace.**
He knew the pain of delay, the weight of injustice, the exhaustion of crisis.
And yet, **he did not lose heart.**

David's life reveals a critical truth about resilience:
Courage is not the absence of fear — it is trusting God in the middle of fear.

Psalm 27:1 declares:

"The Lord is my light and my salvation — whom shall I fear? The Lord is the stronghold of my life — of whom shall I be afraid?" (Psalm 27:1, NIV)

David's courage came not from his circumstances — they were often bleak —
but from his confidence in God's character.

When enemies closed in, David worshiped.
When friends betrayed him, David sought the Lord.
When the promise seemed delayed, David remained faithful.

His resilience was not passive.
David strengthened himself in the Lord (1 Samuel 30:6).
He refused to let fear dictate his future.
He trusted that the God who anointed him would appoint the time for him to reign.

Life Application

There will be seasons when the promises over your life seem delayed, even dead.
Seasons where crisis and chaos shout louder than calling.

In those moments, remember David:

- Strengthen yourself in the Lord.
- Trust God's timing over your own.
- Remain faithful when the wilderness stretches longer than expected.

Resilience is not rushing God's process — it's trusting His plan even when the path is dark.

Declaration of Resilience

Today, I declare:
"The Lord is my light and my salvation.
Fear has no hold on me.
Delay is not denial, and detours do not destroy destiny.
I trust God's timing and His perfect plan for my life.
In Jesus' name, Amen."

Prayer

Father God,
When fear rises, be my strength.
When crisis surrounds me, be my refuge.
Teach me to trust You in the waiting, to find courage in Your promises, and to rest in Your perfect timing.
Strengthen my spirit as You did David's, and help me endure the wilderness seasons with faith and hope.
In Jesus' name, Amen.

Resilience Challenge

- Identify one area where you feel fear or discouragement today.
- Write a prayer of surrender — giving that fear to God.
- Speak Psalm 27:1 aloud:
  "The Lord is the stronghold of my life — of whom shall I be afraid?"

Reflections: David

Take a few moments to reflect on what God has spoken to you through this chapter.

- What is one lesson from David's life that you can apply to your current situation?
- Where is God calling you to have courage in the face of fear?
- What personal declaration can you make based on David's journey of resilience?

Chapter 4: Esther — Risk with Righteousness

Pillar of Resilience: Courage to Stand When It Matters Most

Imagine being a young woman thrust into the heart of a foreign palace.
You are crowned queen, but your people are marked for death. Speaking up could cost you your life. Staying silent could cost countless others theirs.

Esther was faced with a choice that tested the very core of her faith:
Risk everything — or risk losing everything.

Her story reveals another critical truth about resilience:
Resilient faith does not run from risk — it rises with righteousness.

When her uncle Mordecai sent word of the coming destruction, he challenged her:

"And who knows but that you have come to your royal position for such a time as this?" (Esther 4:14, NIV)

Esther's resilience was not born of arrogance or recklessness.
It was born of obedience.
She recognized that her position was not for her comfort, but for God's purpose.

Esther fasted. She prayed. She prepared.
And then she stepped forward with trembling hands but unwavering trust.

Her boldness saved a nation.

Esther's life reminds us that resilience often looks like **standing** when it would be easier to sit.
Speaking when silence feels safer.
Trusting when the future feels uncertain.

Life Application

There will be times when resilience requires you to risk:

- Risk your comfort for your calling.
- Risk your popularity for your convictions.
- Risk your safety for the sake of others.

Resilience doesn't mean you're unafraid — it means you move forward *despite* fear, trusting in a God who holds the outcome.

When God places you in a position of influence — whether great or small — He expects you to use it for His glory.

Declaration of Resilience

Today, I declare:
"I was created for such a time as this.
I will stand in courage and walk in obedience.
Fear will not silence my faith.
God has prepared me for this moment, and I will move forward in His strength.
In Jesus' name, Amen."

Prayer

Father God,
When I feel fear rising, remind me of Your call on my life.
Give me the courage to stand when it would be easier to stay silent.
Teach me to trust not in my own strength, but in Your sovereignty.
Use my life — my position, my voice, my obedience — to accomplish Your purpose.
In Jesus' name, Amen.

Resilience Challenge

- Identify one area where God may be calling you to take a stand.
- Fast and pray like Esther — set aside a day to seek God's wisdom.
- Speak Esther 4:14 aloud:
  "Who knows but that you have come to your royal position for such a time as this?"

Reflections: Esther

Take a few moments to reflect on what God has spoken to you through this chapter.

- What is one lesson from Esther's life that you can apply to your current situation?
- Where is God calling you to stand boldly in faith despite the risks?
- What personal declaration can you make based on Esther's journey of resilience?

Chapter 5: Paul — Strength Under Pressure

Pillar of Resilience: Pressing On When Life Pushes Back

Imagine being beaten, imprisoned, shipwrecked, and left for dead — not once, but multiple times.
Imagine pouring out your life in service to God, only to be misunderstood, persecuted, and abandoned.

Paul lived this reality.
He faced constant pressure, yet never gave up.
His life echoes a powerful truth about resilience:
It's not about avoiding pressure — it's about pressing on under it.

In 2 Corinthians 4:8-9, Paul writes:

"We are hard pressed on every side, but not crushed; perplexed, but not in despair; persecuted, but not abandoned; struck down, but not destroyed." (NIV)

Paul didn't deny his hardships — he acknowledged them.
But he refused to be defined by them.

Paul's resilience wasn't grounded in human strength — it was grounded in *divine purpose*.
He understood that **pressure produces perseverance**, and perseverance produces character, and character produces hope (Romans 5:3-5).

For Paul, resilience was not optional — it was essential to fulfilling his calling.

Life Application

There will be seasons when life feels relentless — when pressures mount from every side.
You will be tempted to quit, to settle, to walk away.

Paul's life teaches us:

- Don't quit when it's hard.
- Don't back down when it's painful.
- Don't give up when progress seems slow.

Resilience is about pressing on — not because it's easy, but because the *calling* is worth it.

Declaration of Resilience

Today, I declare:
"I am pressed, but not crushed.
Persecuted, but not abandoned.
Struck down, but not destroyed.
God's strength is perfected in my weakness.
I will press on toward the goal set before me.
In Jesus' name, Amen."

Prayer

Father God,
When pressure weighs heavy, lift my eyes to You.
When trials surround me, surround me with Your peace.
Strengthen my heart to endure, and my spirit to press on.

Remind me that Your power is made perfect in my weakness.
Help me run my race with endurance, looking to Jesus, the author and finisher of my faith.
In Jesus' name, Amen.

Resilience Challenge

- Identify one area where you feel pressure today.
- Write down how God has sustained you in past pressures.
- Speak 2 Corinthians 4:8-9 aloud:
  "We are hard pressed on every side, but not crushed..."

Reflections: Paul

Take a few moments to reflect on what God has spoken to you through this chapter.

- What is one lesson from Paul's life that you can apply to your current situation?
- Where is God asking you to persevere under pressure?
- What personal declaration can you make based on Paul's journey of resilience?

Chapter 6: Ruth — Loyalty in Loss

Pillar of Resilience: Faithfulness in Uncertainty

Imagine losing everything you once held dear — your husband, your future, your sense of belonging.
In a time of famine and grief, Ruth stood at a crossroads.
She could return to what was familiar and safe, or she could cling to an uncertain future with Naomi — a future built solely on loyalty and faith.

Ruth chose loyalty.
She chose resilience.

Her words to Naomi echo through the ages as a testament to unshakable faith:

"Where you go I will go, and where you stay I will stay. Your people will be my people and your God my God." (Ruth 1:16, NIV)

Ruth didn't know what lay ahead.
She had no guarantees of provision, no clear plan for her future.
But she remained faithful — to Naomi, to her new path, and ultimately to God.

Ruth's story reminds us of a vital truth about resilience:
Faithfulness is powerful, even when the future is uncertain.

Ruth gleaned in fields she did not own.
She served quietly, humbly, consistently.
And God honored her resilience — turning her loss into legacy.

She became the great-grandmother of King David and part of the lineage of Jesus Himself.

Life Application

There will be seasons where life feels stripped down —
Where you face uncertainty, grief, or unexpected endings.

Ruth teaches us:

- Stay faithful even when the way forward is unclear.
- Serve diligently even when no one is watching.
- Trust that God writes beautiful stories from broken beginnings.

Resilience is not always loud; sometimes it is the quiet, daily choice to remain faithful.

Declaration of Resilience

Today, I declare:
"I will be faithful in the unknown.
I will trust God when the path is hidden.
My loyalty is to God's purpose, and my faithfulness will not fail.
He is writing a greater story through my life.
In Jesus' name, Amen."

Prayer

Father God,
When loss and uncertainty cloud my path, help me cling to You. Teach me to be faithful in the small things, to trust You in the unknown, and to serve with humility and hope.
Let my loyalty to You produce fruit beyond what I can see today. Write my story with Your perfect hand.
In Jesus' name, Amen.

Resilience Challenge

- Write down one area of your life where you are tempted to give up because the future seems unclear.
- Commit it to God in prayer today.
- Speak Ruth 1:16 aloud:
  "Where you go I will go, and where you stay I will stay..."

Reflections: Ruth

Take a few moments to reflect on what God has spoken to you through this chapter.

- What is one lesson from Ruth's life that you can apply to your current situation?
- Where is God calling you to stay faithful even when the way forward is uncertain?
- What personal declaration can you make based on Ruth's journey of resilience?

Chapter 7: Daniel — Integrity Under Fire

Pillar of Resilience: Standing Firm in a Shifting Culture

Imagine being taken from your homeland, forced into a foreign culture, given a new name, and pressured to compromise your deepest beliefs.
The easier path would be to blend in — to adapt, to conform, to survive by surrendering.

But Daniel chose a different path.
He chose resilience through integrity.

Daniel's life teaches us a timeless truth:
Resilient faith stands firm when the world bows low.

When a royal decree demanded that no one pray to anyone but the king, Daniel could have complied quietly.
Instead, he opened his windows, knelt down, and prayed — just as he had always done.

Daniel 6:10 records:

"Now when Daniel learned that the decree had been published, he went home to his upstairs room where the windows opened toward Jerusalem. Three times a day he got down on his knees and prayed, giving thanks to his God, just as he had done before." (NIV)

Daniel understood that resilience sometimes means refusing to bow — even when it costs you everything.

His integrity led him to a lions' den —
but his faith led him through it, untouched and unafraid.

In a culture that constantly shifts, Daniel's unwavering stand shows us that true resilience is *not bending under pressure*, but *standing firm in truth*.

Life Application

We live in a world where truth is often relative, and compromise is expected.
Resilient faith demands:

- Standing for God's truth even when it's unpopular.
- Living with integrity even when no one is watching.
- Choosing obedience over acceptance.

Resilience is not just enduring hardship — it's remaining *unchanged* by the culture around you.

Declaration of Resilience

Today, I declare:
"I will stand firm in my faith.
I will not bow to fear, compromise, or pressure.
My integrity will shine like a light in darkness.
I will remain faithful, no matter the cost.
In Jesus' name, Amen."

Prayer

Father God,
In a world that shifts and bends, make me steadfast.
Give me the courage to stand for You when compromise calls.
Strengthen my integrity when pressure mounts.
Let my life be a testimony to Your unchanging truth and unfailing love.
In Jesus' name, Amen.

Resilience Challenge

- Identify one area where you are tempted to compromise your integrity.
- Commit to standing firm this week, even in small things.
- Speak Daniel 6:10 aloud:
  "He got down on his knees and prayed, giving thanks to his God, just as he had done before."

Reflections: Daniel

Take a few moments to reflect on what God has spoken to you through this chapter.

- What is one lesson from Daniel's life that you can apply to your current situation?
- Where is God calling you to stand firm in your convictions?
- What personal declaration can you make based on Daniel's journey of resilience?

Chapter 8: Nehemiah — Vision Amid Opposition

Pillar of Resilience: Building Despite Criticism

Imagine feeling the burden to rebuild what others had long abandoned.
The walls of Jerusalem lay in ruins — a symbol of disgrace and defeat. Nehemiah, though comfortable in the king's palace, carried the vision to restore what was broken.

But no great work is without great opposition.

Nehemiah's story teaches a powerful truth about resilience:
When you pursue God's vision, expect resistance — but build anyway.

In Nehemiah 4:6, despite threats and mockery from his enemies, it says:

"So we rebuilt the wall till all of it reached half its height, for the people worked with all their heart." (NIV)

Nehemiah faced constant criticism and sabotage attempts:

- *"What are these feeble Jews doing?"* (Nehemiah 4:2)
- Threats of attack.
- False accusations.

But Nehemiah didn't come down from the wall.
He didn't waste time arguing with critics — he stayed focused on the mission God had given him.

Nehemiah shows us that **resilience means pressing forward even when people misunderstand you, oppose you, or try to distract you.**

He prayed. He planned. He persisted.
And in just 52 days, the walls were rebuilt.

Life Application

When you pursue a God-given dream, not everyone will support you. Some will doubt you. Others will oppose you outright.

Nehemiah's resilience teaches:

- Stay focused on what God called you to build.
- Pray through opposition, but don't quit because of it.
- Trust that God's assignment is bigger than people's opinions.

Resilience is not just about surviving attacks — it's about *thriving in spite of them.*

Declaration of Resilience

Today, I declare:
"I will not come down from the wall God has called me to build.
Criticism will not distract me.
Fear will not derail me.
My focus is on God's purpose, and I will finish the work He has given me.
In Jesus' name, Amen."

Prayer

Father God,
When opposition rises, anchor me in Your truth.
Strengthen my hands for the work You have assigned to me.
Let no voice of fear or criticism pull me away from Your purpose.
Help me build faithfully and finish strong.
In Jesus' name, Amen.

Resilience Challenge

- Write down a vision or goal you believe God has placed on your heart.
- List one distraction or criticism that has tried to pull you off course.
- Speak Nehemiah 4:6 aloud:
  "We rebuilt the wall till all of it reached half its height, for the people worked with all their heart."

Reflections: Nehemiah

Take a few moments to reflect on what God has spoken to you through this chapter.

- What is one lesson from Nehemiah's life that you can apply to your current situation?
- Where is God calling you to stay focused despite distractions and criticism?
- What personal declaration can you make based on Nehemiah's journey of resilience?

Chapter 9: Hannah — Patient Hope

Pillar of Resilience: Trusting God's Timing

Imagine longing for something so deeply it consumes your prayers, your thoughts, your dreams — year after year.
Hannah longed for a child, but her womb remained closed.
She endured not just the ache of unanswered prayers, but also the taunts of her rival and the misunderstanding of others.

Still, Hannah did not let disappointment define her.

Hannah's life teaches a powerful truth about resilience:
Real hope is not passive — it is persistent.

1 Samuel 1:10-11 paints a picture of her pain and perseverance:

"In her deep anguish Hannah prayed to the Lord, weeping bitterly. And she made a vow, saying, 'Lord Almighty, if you will only look on your servant's misery and remember me...then I will give him to the Lord for all the days of his life.'" (NIV)

Hannah didn't give up.
She brought her broken heart to the altar — not once, but continually.
She trusted that even in delay, God was working.

Her patient hope birthed not only her son Samuel, who would become a mighty prophet, but also a legacy of faithfulness.

Hannah's resilience shows us that **waiting is not wasting** — and that God's "no" today may be preparing the way for a bigger "yes" tomorrow.

Life Application

Waiting seasons can feel like wilderness seasons — dry, lonely, and endless.
But God uses the wait to shape our character, refine our desires, and align our hearts with His will.

Hannah teaches us:

- Bring your pain to God, not away from Him.
- Be faithful in the waiting.
- Trust that God's timing is never late — it's always perfect.

Resilience is trusting that *God's delays are not His denials.*

Declaration of Resilience

Today, I declare:
"My hope is in the Lord.
I trust His timing over my own.
Delayed answers do not mean forgotten prayers.
God is working in the waiting, and I will patiently hope in Him.
In Jesus' name, Amen."

Prayer

Father God,
In seasons of delay and silence, anchor my heart in Your faithfulness.
Teach me to hope patiently, to pray persistently, and to trust wholeheartedly.
Remind me that You hear every prayer and collect every tear.
Strengthen me to wait well, knowing that Your plans for me are good.
In Jesus' name, Amen.

Resilience Challenge

- Identify an area of your life where you are still waiting for an answer.
- Spend time in prayer today, not just for the answer, but for peace in the process.
- Speak 1 Samuel 1:10 aloud:
  "In her deep anguish Hannah prayed to the Lord, weeping bitterly."

Reflections: Hannah

Take a few moments to reflect on what God has spoken to you through this chapter.

- What is one lesson from Hannah's life that you can apply to your current situation?
- Where is God asking you to hope patiently in the waiting?
- What personal declaration can you make based on Hannah's journey of resilience?

Chapter 10: Peter — Restoration After Failure

Pillar of Resilience: Rising After Falling

Imagine walking with Jesus, witnessing miracles, and pledging your loyalty with boldness.
Imagine, too, the crushing shame of denying Him — not once, but three times — in His greatest hour of need.
Peter knew the sting of failure.

But Peter also knew the beauty of restoration.

Peter's life teaches a powerful truth about resilience:
Failure is not final when grace is in the story.

After His resurrection, Jesus didn't shame Peter — He restored him. In John 21:15-17, Jesus asks Peter three times, *"Do you love Me?"* — one affirmation for every denial.
Then He recommissions him:

"Feed My sheep." (John 21:17, NIV)

Peter's resilience was not in pretending he hadn't failed.
It was in **accepting grace** and **rising again**.

He went on to become a bold leader in the early church, preaching at Pentecost where thousands were saved — the same Peter who once cowered before a servant girl.

Peter's story reminds us that **resilient faith doesn't deny failure — it overcomes it**.

In God's hands, even our deepest failures can become the foundation for our greatest callings.

Life Application

You will fall.
You will fail.
But failure is not the end of your story — not with Jesus.

Peter teaches us:

- Own your failures — but don't live in them.
- Accept the grace Jesus offers.
- Step back into your calling with humility and boldness.

Resilience is not about never falling — it's about *always getting back up*.

Declaration of Resilience

Today, I declare:
"My failures do not define me.
God's grace restores me.
I will rise, I will walk in forgiveness, and I will fulfill the calling God has placed on my life.
In Jesus' name, Amen."

Prayer

Father God,
When I stumble, lift me up.
When I fail, remind me of Your restoring grace.
Heal the places of shame in my heart and restore me to bold, faithful service.
Help me to rise stronger, love deeper, and walk humbly in the calling You've given me.
In Jesus' name, Amen.

Resilience Challenge

- Reflect on an area where you have failed or fallen.
- Write down one lesson God has taught you through that failure.
- Speak John 21:17 aloud:
  "Feed My sheep." — a reminder that your calling still stands.

Reflections: Peter

Take a few moments to reflect on what God has spoken to you through this chapter.

- What is one lesson from Peter's life that you can apply to your current situation?
- Where is God calling you to rise again after failure?
- What personal declaration can you make based on Peter's journey of resilience?

Chapter 11: Moses — Leadership in the Wilderness

Pillar of Resilience: Enduring While Waiting

Imagine being called by God to lead an entire nation to freedom. Now imagine spending 40 years wandering through the wilderness with people who complained, doubted, rebelled, and resisted at every turn.

Moses knew the weight of leadership.
He knew the pain of delayed promises.
And yet, Moses remained faithful to the call — even when the journey was far longer and harder than he ever expected.

Moses' life teaches a powerful truth about resilience:
Leadership is not just about starting strong — it's about enduring to the finish.

Hebrews 11:27 speaks of Moses' endurance:

"By faith he left Egypt, not fearing the king's anger; he persevered because he saw Him who is invisible." (NIV)

Moses endured:

- The impatience of the people.
- The loneliness of leadership.
- The disappointment of seeing the Promised Land from a distance but not entering it.

Yet he remained faithful — not because the journey was easy, but because the One who called him was worthy.

Moses teaches us that **true resilience is found in staying faithful during the long, hard seasons** — especially when the finish line feels far away.

Life Application

Leadership — whether in ministry, family, or community — often means enduring:

- Delays that test your patience.
- People who test your character.
- Challenges that test your commitment.

Moses reminds us:

- Don't let delays discourage you.
- Don't let difficulties disqualify you.
- Keep walking — even when the wilderness feels endless.

Resilience is not just starting with fire — it's finishing with faithfulness.

Declaration of Resilience

Today, I declare:
"I will endure the wilderness with faith.
I will lead with patience and finish with perseverance.
God's promises are worth the wait.
I will not give up before the breakthrough.
In Jesus' name, Amen."

Prayer

Father God,
Strengthen my heart to lead well, even in the wilderness.
Teach me to trust Your timing, to endure with hope, and to walk with patience.
Help me to persevere when the journey is long and the destination seems distant.
Let my life and leadership bring You glory.
In Jesus' name, Amen.

Resilience Challenge

- Reflect on an area of leadership in your life — home, work, ministry.
- Identify one way you can endure with greater patience this week.
- Speak Hebrews 11:27 aloud:
  "He persevered because he saw Him who is invisible."

Reflections: Moses

Take a few moments to reflect on what God has spoken to you through this chapter.

- What is one lesson from Moses's life that you can apply to your current situation?
- Where is God calling you to lead with endurance during long seasons?
- What personal declaration can you make based on Moses's journey of resilience?

Chapter 12: Jesus — Endurance for Glory

Pillar of Resilience: Persevering for the Greater Joy

Imagine carrying the weight of the world's sin on your shoulders. Imagine being betrayed by a friend, abandoned by those closest to you, beaten, mocked, and crucified — all while possessing the power to stop it.

Jesus endured it all.

His life — and His death — teach the ultimate truth about resilience: **Endurance is not just about surviving — it's about pressing on for a greater glory.**

Hebrews 12:2 gives us the key to Jesus' endurance:

"For the joy set before Him, He endured the cross, scorning its shame, and sat down at the right hand of the throne of God." (NIV)

Jesus didn't endure the cross because it was easy — He endured because of the *joy* on the other side:

- The joy of redeeming humanity.
- The joy of reconciling us to the Father.
- The joy of fulfilling the mission He was sent to accomplish.

Jesus shows us that **resilience reaches its highest form when it's fueled by purpose.**

When you have a *why* that is bigger than the pain, you can endure *anything*.

For Jesus, *we* were the "why."
For us, *He* is the reason we can endure.

Life Application

You will face trials that feel unbearable.
But when you set your eyes on joy beyond the pain — the greater purpose — you find strength to endure.

Jesus teaches us:

- Don't quit in the pain — look to the promise.
- Endurance has a reward.
- Glory always follows suffering for those who trust God.

Resilience is not blind toughness — it's *purposeful perseverance*.

Declaration of Resilience

Today, I declare:
"I fix my eyes on Jesus, the author and finisher of my faith.
I will endure hardship for the joy set before me.
My pain is temporary, but my purpose is eternal.
I will finish my race strong, to the glory of God.
In Jesus' name, Amen."

Prayer

Father God,
When the road is hard and the cross is heavy, fix my eyes on Jesus.
Teach me to endure with joy, to persevere with purpose, and to trust that glory lies ahead.
Give me the strength to carry my cross and the courage to finish my race.
Thank You for the example of Jesus — my Savior, my Strength, and my Song.
In His mighty name, Amen.

Resilience Challenge

- Reflect on a trial you are enduring right now.
- Ask God to give you a vision of the "joy set before you" — the purpose beyond the pain.
- Speak Hebrews 12:2 aloud:
  "For the joy set before Him, He endured the cross."

Reflections: Jesus

Take a few moments to reflect on what God has spoken to you through this chapter.

- What is one lesson from Jesus's life that you can apply to your current situation?
- Where is God asking you to endure for the greater joy ahead?
- What personal declaration can you make based on Jesus's journey of resilience?

Conclusion: Living a Resilient Faith

Resilience is more than grit.
It is more than stubborn determination.
It is more than the ability to survive difficult seasons.

Resilient faith is *trusting God through the storm.*
It is *standing firm when everything else shakes.*
It is *rising again when life knocks you down.*
It is *pressing forward when the world says quit.*

The stories of Joseph, Job, David, Esther, Paul, Ruth, Daniel, Nehemiah, Hannah, Peter, Moses, and Jesus were not written to decorate the pages of history.
They were written to ignite courage in you.

Their battles were real. Their struggles were fierce. Their doubts and delays were just as painful as ours.
But **they endured** — not because they were perfect, but because **God is faithful**.

You, too, are called to resilient faith.
A faith that:

- Stands when others fall.
- Endures when others walk away.
- Hopes when all seems lost.
- Believes when the waiting feels endless.
- Loves when it hurts.
- Trusts when it's dark.

The road will not always be easy.
The cost will sometimes be high.
But the reward — the *joy set before you* — will be worth every step.

Your Journey Forward

As you close this book, this is not the end — it's your beginning.

Take the lessons of these 12 lives and live them out:

- Stand strong like Joseph, even in betrayal.
- Worship like Job, even in suffering.
- Lead like David, even in hiding.
- Speak boldly like Esther, even at risk.
- Endure like Paul, even when pressed on every side.
- Stay faithful like Ruth, even in loss.
- Stand firm like Daniel, even in a shifting culture.
- Build like Nehemiah, even amid opposition.
- Wait like Hannah, even in silence.
- Rise like Peter, even after failure.
- Lead like Moses, even through the wilderness.
- Endure like Jesus, even to the cross — and beyond it.

You were not created for defeat.
You were created to **overcome**.
You were made for **resilient faith**.

"Blessed is the one who perseveres under trial because, having stood the test, that person will receive the crown of life that the Lord has promised to those who love Him."
— James 1:12 (NIV)

Final Resilience Challenge

- Write your own declaration of resilient faith.
- Speak it aloud every morning for the next 30 days.
- Commit to living a life that stands as a testament to God's faithfulness.

Commissioning Prayer

Father God,
I thank You for the stories that inspire me and the Spirit that empowers me.
Plant in me a faith that endures, a hope that refuses to quit, and a love that stands unshaken.
Strengthen my hands when they grow weary.
Steady my heart when the path feels long.
Let my life reflect Your glory, and let my resilience point others to Your greatness.
I am not alone. I am not defeated. I am not abandoned.
I am resilient — because You are faithful.
In Jesus' mighty name, Amen.

7-Day Resilience Devotional

Building Endurance One Day at a Time

Day 1: Strength in Weakness

Scripture

"But He said to me, 'My grace is sufficient for you, for My power is made perfect in weakness.' Therefore I will boast all the more gladly about my weaknesses, so that Christ's power may rest on me."
— 2 Corinthians 12:9 (NIV)

Devotional

Resilience often feels like strength — but the foundation of true resilience is recognizing that **our strength is not enough**.
God never intended for you to face battles in your own power.
He allows weakness to remind you of His sufficiency.

Paul, one of the most resilient men in Scripture, was not boasting about his strength, but about his **weakness**.
Why?
Because it was in his weakness that God's power was most visible.

In seasons when you feel inadequate, depleted, or overwhelmed — remember:
God's grace is sufficient.
His power shines brightest when we can no longer rely on ourselves.

True resilience is not self-reliance — it is God-dependence.

Reflection

- In what areas of your life do you feel the most weak or stretched right now?
- How might God want to show His power through your weakness?

Declaration

Today, I declare:
"I will not be defeated by weakness.
God's grace is sufficient for me.
His power is made perfect in my weakness.
I stand strong in Him.
In Jesus' name, Amen."

Prayer

Father God,
Thank You that I do not have to be strong in myself.
Teach me to lean fully on Your grace.
In moments of weakness, remind me that Your power is made perfect in me.
Help me walk in humble dependence and confident trust.
Let Your strength be seen in my life today.
In Jesus' name, Amen.

Today's Challenge

- Write down one area where you feel weak or incapable.
- Pray specifically for God's grace and strength in that area today.

Day 2: Courage to Keep Going

Scripture

"Have I not commanded you? Be strong and courageous. Do not be afraid; do not be discouraged, for the Lord your God will be with you wherever you go."
— Joshua 1:9 (NIV)

Devotional

Fear is a natural response when the future looks uncertain. Discouragement easily creeps in when progress feels slow and obstacles seem overwhelming.

But God's command to Joshua — a leader about to step into the unknown — was clear:
Be strong and courageous.

Courage is not the absence of fear — it's the decision to move forward *in spite of it*.
It's trusting that **God's presence** outweighs any threat ahead.

Resilient faith doesn't wait for the fear to disappear.
It chooses to believe God's promises and keep moving, even with trembling hands and a racing heart.

Joshua succeeded not because the road was easy, but because **the Lord his God was with him**.

The same promise is yours today.

Reflection

- Where are you hesitating because of fear?
- What step of courage is God inviting you to take today?

Declaration

Today, I declare:
"I will be strong and courageous.
Fear will not control me.
Discouragement will not stop me.
The Lord is with me wherever I go.
In Jesus' name, Amen."

Prayer

Father God,
Thank You that I never walk alone.
Fill me with courage to face the battles ahead.
Help me move forward even when fear tries to hold me back.
Remind me that Your presence is my strength and my shield.
I choose courage today — because You are with me.
In Jesus' name, Amen.

Today's Challenge

- Write down one fear that has been holding you back.
- Speak Joshua 1:9 aloud over that fear today:
  "Be strong and courageous. Do not be afraid; do not be discouraged."

Day 3: Endurance in Trials

Scripture

"Blessed is the one who perseveres under trial because, having stood the test, that person will receive the crown of life that the Lord has promised to those who love Him."
— James 1:12 (NIV)

Devotional

Trials test more than your strength — they test your endurance.

When everything in you wants to quit, resilience says, *"Stay the course."*
Not because the trial is easy, but because **the reward is worth it**.

James reminds us that blessing comes not to those who avoid trials, but to those who **persevere through them**.

Endurance isn't passive — it's active trust.
It's choosing to believe that God is working even when you can't see the evidence.
It's holding onto His promises when the pressure increases.

Resilience is not about never feeling tired — it's about refusing to let weariness win.

Today, no matter how heavy the burden or how long the battle, press on.
There is a crown waiting on the other side.

Reflection

- What trial are you currently enduring?
- How can you shift your focus today from the trial itself to the blessing God promises?

Declaration

Today, I declare:
"I will persevere under trial.
God is with me, strengthening me for the journey.
The blessing is ahead, and I will not give up.
My endurance will be rewarded.
In Jesus' name, Amen."

Prayer

Father God,
When the journey is hard and the trials are heavy, sustain me.
Give me the endurance to keep moving forward.
Help me fix my eyes not on the trial, but on the crown of life You have promised.
Strengthen my heart, steady my steps, and renew my hope today.
In Jesus' name, Amen.

Today's Challenge

- Write down James 1:12 and place it somewhere visible — a reminder that endurance brings blessing.
- Pray specifically for renewed strength to endure what you are facing today.

Day 4: Hope in Waiting

Scripture

"But if we hope for what we do not yet have, we wait for it patiently."
— Romans 8:25 (NIV)

Devotional

Waiting tests the soul like few things can.

Waiting feels like silence. Like delay.
Sometimes it feels like God is standing still when we are desperate for Him to move.

But the truth is this: **waiting is not wasted** when God is in it.
He uses seasons of waiting to stretch our faith, deepen our trust, and refine our hearts.

Paul reminds us that real hope is not in what we already see —
it's in what we *know* God will do, even when we can't see it yet.

Hope is the anchor that holds you steady during the wait.
It reminds you that God's promises are certain, even if the timeline is unclear.

Today, don't lose heart because you are waiting.
Stand firm, anchored in the hope that God is working behind the scenes — preparing, shaping, aligning.
His timing is perfect.

Reflection

- In what area of your life are you waiting for God to move?
- How can you strengthen your hope during this season?

Declaration

Today, I declare:
"My hope is anchored in God's promises.
I will wait patiently and trust fully.
What God has spoken, He will bring to pass.
The waiting is preparing me for the blessing.
In Jesus' name, Amen."

Prayer

Father God,
Waiting is hard, but I trust You in it.
Anchor my soul in Your promises.
Strengthen my hope so that I do not grow weary or lose heart.
Remind me daily that Your timing is perfect and that the waiting is not in vain.
Thank You for the work You are doing even when I cannot see it.
In Jesus' name, Amen.

Today's Challenge

- Write down one promise from God's Word that gives you hope.
- Meditate on Romans 8:25 throughout your day:
  "We hope for what we do not yet have, we wait for it patiently."

Day 5: Peace in Pressure

Scripture

"You will keep in perfect peace those whose minds are steadfast, because they trust in You."
— Isaiah 26:3 (NIV)

Devotional

Pressure has a way of pushing us to the edge — rushing our thoughts, stirring our anxieties, and stealing our peace.
In stressful seasons, it's easy to think that peace is found only when the storm ends.

But God's promise is different.
He offers **perfect peace** — not when the pressure is gone, but *in the middle of it*.

Isaiah reminds us that peace is not tied to the absence of problems, but to the presence of **trust**.
When our minds are steadfast — fixed on God, not on the chaos around us — we can experience a peace that doesn't make sense to the world.

Peace in pressure is possible when trust is in place.
Pressure may surround you, but it doesn't have to consume you.

Today, choose to fix your mind on God — and let His peace guard your heart.

Reflection

- What situation in your life is causing you pressure right now?
- How can you intentionally fix your mind on God instead of the problem?

Declaration

Today, I declare:
"I have perfect peace because I trust in God.
Pressure will not break me.
Anxiety will not rule me.
My mind is fixed on the Lord, and His peace guards my heart.
In Jesus' name, Amen."

Prayer

Father God,
Thank You for being my peace in every storm.
Help me to fix my mind on You and not on my circumstances.
When pressure rises, let Your perfect peace rule in my heart.
Teach me to trust You deeper and rest in Your promises.
I receive Your peace today.
In Jesus' name, Amen.

Today's Challenge

- When you feel pressure today, stop and pray Isaiah 26:3 out loud.
- Write down three ways God has been faithful in the past — reminders that you can trust Him now.

Day 6: Joy in Hard Places

Scripture

"Consider it pure joy, my brothers and sisters, whenever you face trials of many kinds, because you know that the testing of your faith produces perseverance."
— James 1:2-3 (NIV)

Devotional

Joy seems like the last thing you would expect in hard places.

Trials are painful. Loss is real. Disappointment hurts.
And yet, James challenges us with this radical truth:
Consider it pure joy — not because the trial is good, but because what the trial *produces* is good.

Joy in hard places is not about pretending everything is fine.
It's about trusting that God is doing a deeper work inside of you.
Testing strengthens your faith.
Trials grow your endurance.
Pain refines your purpose.

Joy is the supernatural confidence that no matter how difficult the season, **God is producing something in you** that is eternal and unshakable.

Today, don't look for a way out of the trial — look for the joy *in* it.
Joy is not a denial of reality — it's a declaration of God's sovereignty.

Reflection

- Where have you struggled to find joy recently?
- What is one thing God may be producing in your life through this trial?

Declaration

Today, I declare:
"I will consider it pure joy when I face trials.
God is producing perseverance and refining my faith.
Joy is my strength, and I will not lose heart.
In Jesus' name, Amen."

Prayer

Father God,
Help me to see joy not just in easy seasons, but in the hard places too.
Open my eyes to the work You are doing in me through every trial.
Strengthen my heart to endure with joy and hope.
Let my life be a testimony that Your joy is greater than my struggles.
In Jesus' name, Amen.

Today's Challenge

- Write down one lesson you are learning through your current trial.
- Thank God specifically for how He is growing you — even before you see the full result.

Day 7: Finishing Strong

Scripture

"I have fought the good fight, I have finished the race, I have kept the faith."
— 2 Timothy 4:7 (NIV)

Devotional

Starting is easy.
Finishing — that's where the battle is won.

Paul, near the end of his life, looked back and declared with confidence:
"I have finished the race."

His life was not without hardship — imprisonment, beatings, betrayal, loss.
But Paul's legacy wasn't measured by how he started — it was marked by how he *finished*.

Resilience is the daily decision to stay faithful to the call, even when it's hard, even when no one notices, even when the results are slow.

God doesn't just call you to begin well — He calls you to finish well.

Today, recommit your heart to the race set before you.
Stay faithful. Stay focused.
Let heaven — not circumstances — be your measure of success.

You are not running alone.
God is running with you — empowering you to finish strong.

Reflection

- In what areas of your life is God calling you to stay the course?
- How can you realign your heart and focus on finishing strong?

Declaration

Today, I declare:
"I will fight the good fight.
I will finish the race.
I will keep the faith.
I am strengthened by God to endure and to finish strong.
In Jesus' name, Amen."

Prayer

Father God,
Thank You for the race You have set before me.
Strengthen my heart to stay faithful to the end.
Help me to run with endurance, to fight the good fight, and to keep the faith.
Let my life glorify You — not just in the beginning, but all the way to the finish line.
In Jesus' name, Amen.

Today's Challenge

✓ **Write a Personal Commitment Statement**

- Take a few minutes to write a **Personal Commitment to Finish Strong**.
- Include what finishing strong looks like for you — in your faith, your relationships, your calling.
- Keep it somewhere you can revisit when the journey gets tough.

Acknowledgments

I am deeply grateful to God, the anchor of my soul and the source of all strength and resilience. Without His unfailing grace, this journey would not have been possible.

To my family and friends, thank you for your unwavering encouragement, prayers, and belief in the work God has called me to do. Your support has carried me through seasons of both challenge and triumph.

To every reader who picks up *Resilient Faith*, my prayer is that these words will ignite courage and renew your hope. May you find strength in every trial and draw closer to the heart of God with each page.

All glory and honor to Him who makes all things possible.

About the Author

Risa Stegall is a Christian author dedicated to encouraging believers to stand firm in faith through life's challenges. With a commitment to biblical truth and spiritual growth, she writes to inspire resilience, hope, and unwavering trust in God's promises.

Resilient Faith reflects her desire to equip readers with timeless principles for navigating hardships with courage and grace.

For inquiries, updates, or future releases, contact:
shepherdsword@shepherdswordpublishing.com

Thank You

Thank you for taking this journey through *Resilient Faith*.

My prayer is that these words have strengthened your heart and encouraged your spirit to trust God more deeply, no matter what challenges you face.

May His grace sustain you, and may your faith grow stronger with each step you take.

To God be the glory.

www.ingramcontent.com/pod-product-compliance
Lightning Source LLC
Chambersburg PA
CBHW071235090426
42736CB00014B/3085